THE DREAM GARDENER

A Story for Children of All Ages from Five to One Hundred and Five

Written by Andrew Ramer
Illustrated by Jack Ramer

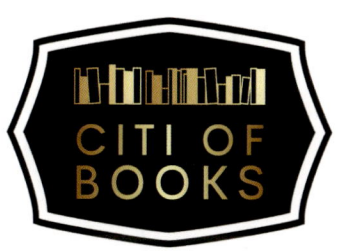

CITI OF BOOKS

CITIOFBOOKS, INC.
3736 Eubank NE Suite A1
Albuquerque, NM 87111-3579
www.citiofbooks.com
Hotline: 1 (877) 389-2759
Fax: 1 (505) 930-7244

Ordering Information:
Quantity sales. Special discounts are available on quantity purchases by corporations, associations, and others. For details, contact the publisher at the address above.

Printed in the United States of America.

ISBN-13:	Softcover	979-8-89391-435-1
	Hardcover	979-8-89391-436-8
	eBook	979-8-89391-437-5

Library of Congress Control Number: 2024923890

The Dream Garden-
er

by

andrew ramer

illustrated

by

jack ramer

Books by Andrew Ramer

Ever After
Two Flutes Playing
Two Hearts Dancing
Our Tribe Chanting
Texting with Angels
Fragments of the Brooklyn Talmud
Deathless
Torah Told Different
Queering the Text
Angel Answers
Revelations for a New Millennium

with Donna Cunningham:

The Spiritual Dimensions of Healing Addictions
Further Dimensions of Healing Addictions

with Alma Daniel and Timothy Wyllie:

Ask Your Angels

The dream gardener plants dreams
in the dream garden.

Each morning he hoes the soil
and plants the small clear seeds in rows.
He waters them
and watches the new plants grow.
By noon the shoots are standing straight and tall.
By sunset the shimmering dream flowers
are fully grown and beginning to drift off
into the world,
each one carrying inside
another dream
for someone else to dream
that night.

The dream gardener
has been doing his work for years and years.
Your parents, your grandparents,
and their parents too,
dreamed dreams that he planted
in his garden
at the far edge of the world.
But sometimes,
when he lies awake in bed,
listening to the sounds
that drift up into his garden
he is sad.
Because all the drifting flowers from his garden
look the same.
But some bring dreamers happy dreams,
and others carry nightmares instead.

One night
the crying scream of a child out in the world,
perhaps it was you,
was so upsetting to the dream gardener
that he sat up in his bed,
turned on the light,
frightened
as if it had been his own nightmare,
and said,
"From this time forward
I will never plant
another dream seed again."

Next morning the dream gardener got up
went out into the garden
and planted ordinary flower seeds,
big seeds and small ones,
but not a single dream seed.

That evening,
sitting comfortably on his porch
with a steaming cup of tea
and a plate of cookies
on the table in front of him
he was happy.
"No one will wake up
in the dark
afraid and crying,
calling out for their parents
ever again."

And that night,
snug in his cozy bed
he listened for sounds of crying
but there were none.
And he himself slept soundly, soundly, soundly
until the sun came up.

The next afternoon
he was trimming the hedges in his garden
when he noticed something curious
coming up the slopes
toward his garden.
It wasn't a sound,
it wasn't a smell,
it just a feeling,
a sense,
not that anything was wrong,
but that something
something wasn't quite right.

And the day after that, the funny feeling
was stronger yet,
like the odor of something unpleasant
coming up over the hills,
cold and wet.
But the nights were quiet.
No one woke up scared,
and the dream gardener
in his bed,
slept happily for hours.

At the end of the week
the feeling
was stronger than ever.
And now it came with the sounds
of irritation
of upset,
and anger.
He could hear doors banging
down in the world,
hear pencils snapping
and someone's coffee mug
hurled across the room.
He put down the packet
of petunia seeds he was planting
to listen to the sound
of your mother,
annoyed at you
and sounding cranky.

The crankiness continued.
Soon, it was all over the world,
the sounds of people getting nasty,
yelling at family and friends,
at other shoppers,
and even at their favorite store clerks.

"This is not good,"
the dream gardener said.
"Something is wrong in the world."
He could hear Tommy,
teasing his tabby cat Griselda.
Then he heard Griselda meowing
as Tommy tugged on her tail.
And heard Sarah
pouring water in a pail
that she tossed
with a mean laugh
all over her baby sister Gail.

Although the sounds were upsetting
they came from far away.
Everything was peaceful in the dream garden
and the dream gardener spent his days
planting roses and lilies,
tulips, crocuses, and hyacinths,
and all the flowers
he'd never had time to plant
since the day he took over the garden from his mother,
who took it over from hers.
In fact
his family had been planting dream flowers for so long
that he couldn't remember
where the first seeds came from,
or when the garden began.

And that night in his bed,
the world was oh so quiet.
"I could come to like this,"
said the gardener,
as if he'd been put on
an ice cream and cookies diet.
Yes, the nights were still,
no nightmares – anywhere.
But each day was noisier than the one before it.
Down in the world
all he could hear were the sounds
of anger,
of anger and fear.

Soon horns were blasting,
and people were screaming at each other.
Fathers were fighting with their children,
and sisters and brothers
were hitting and yelling
and breaking each other's things.
All of those sounds
came echoing up into the dream garden,
Its unplanted dream seeds,
sitting in burlap sacks
in a rickety old shed.
"Oh my, oh my,"
said the gardener,
"this is worse
than any nightmare."

But that night it was quiet,
and the gardener slept well again,
but he put cotton in his ears
as he worked in his fields.
But no cotton could silence
the booming
coming up from the world.

Just before dawn
the gardener was awakened,
by such a thunderous noise
coming into the garden
that he couldn't hear himself think at all.
And for the first time
it occurred to him
that all of this noise in the world
began soon after he stopped planting dreams.
So he leaped out of bed
grabbed his shirt and pants,
from a chair at the foot in the corner,
jumped into them,
put on his socks and shoes,
and raced out into the garden..

As fast as he could
the gardener ran
to the little shed
at the edge of the trees
where he stored his unused dream seeds.
As he raced
the noises from the world
were so loud
that he had to put his hands on his ears.
But that didn't block out.
The booming and crashing.
The screaming and wailing.
The sobbing.
But with a sack over his shoulder
and a rake in one hand
he ran out to an unused plot of earth
turned the soil
and started planting.

Row after row he planted,
as fast as he could,
tossing hands full of clear dream seeds
into the dry brown earth.
Then he filled up his watering can
and marched up and down the rows
watering the seeds he planted,
happy to see the dry soil darkening.
And because they were dream seeds
they soon began to sprout,
but the noises from the world were so loud,
loud of screaming and shouting
that the gardener despaired
of what might happen
down there
in the world.

But by noon
the dark green stalks were growing tall
and then tiny dream flowers began to emerge
at the ends of every stalk.
And by sunset,
the sky painted coral and gold
hundreds of dream flowers
started to float
across the fields
sparkling, shimmering,
then they rose up into the sky
carrying dreams,
good dreams and bad dreams
up and out into the world.

Exhausted,
the dream gardener
collapsed into a chair.
He hardly slept at all that night,
listening.
Not sure if he could hear
any difference in the sounds
coming up to him
from the world.

But the next day
the world was quieter.
The gardener could tell.
And he planted new dream seeds
certain
that his work was making a difference.
And that night
just as he turned off his bedroom light
he could hear the cry of a little child
waking up from a bad dream.
And the dream gardener
fell asleep again.
Happy.
Knowing that we need good dreams to cheer us
and bad dreams to release
the upsets that we carry.
That if we don't have them
we feel worse and worse.

In a few days
the world was back to normal.
And the dream gardener
stopped one morning
at the edge of his fields
to enjoy all the sounds
that came up to him from the world.
Then he grabbed his rake,
grabbed a sack of dream seeds,
and began to plant them.
As he does every day now.
Every day.

The End

Afterword

The story you just read was written around 1975. When I finished it I showed it to my father Jack, who did the illustrations. Dad was an architect, artist, playwright, and also a gifted musician who would strap his harmonica on his head and play it and his guitar at the same time.

When Dad died in 1980, two days after his fifty-seventh birthday, I stuck the story away and forgot about it for – forty-four years! Then one afternoon I was going through boxes of old letters and manuscripts – and there was **The Dream Gardener** – sitting in a manila file folder.

Although long out of print, my very first book, *little pictures: fiction for a new age*, published in 1987, is a collection of very short stories that I did the illustrations for myself. (They're black-and-white and not nearly as good as Dad's!) That book's original subtitle was *bedtime stories for grownups,* but **The Dream Gardener** is a book for kids and grownups too. I hope you liked it!

I was born in 1951 in Elm/hurst, Queens, New York, right across the street from an amusement park called Fairyland, and now I live in Oak/Land, California, up the street from an amusement park called Fairyland. A lover of fairies, fairy tales, trees, and the books that come from them, the slash marks in those locations are deliberate.

For more information on my books and other writing, please visit my website: andrewramer.com

Acknowledgments

Thank you Dad, Jack, Yankel - for the dreams you shared,
the art and music you shared, and for illuminating my little story so
beautifully. I wish you'd gotten to see it and hold it in your amazingly
creative hands.

I would like to thank my architect brother Richard
and his artist wife Lisa for your support of this project.
You can read about their work at: ramer.com and lisaocchipinti.com

And I celebrate the ones who call me Papa, Dad, Saba - David-Michael, John,
Jasminder, Patanjali, Jesse, Estrella, and Levi.

With deep gratitude to everyone at CITI OF BOOKS, including Sebastian
Mercer, Chloe Bennett, Talia Davis, and Kelsey Marquez.